AUG - 6 2019

W9-AUM-640

THE GRIFFIN POETRY PRIZE
Anthology 2019

Copyright © 2019 House of Anansi Press Inc.
Poems copyright © Individual poets
Preface copyright © Kim Maltman

Published in Canada in 2019 and the USA in 2019 by House of Anansi Press Inc.
www.houseofanansi.com

All rights reserved. No part of this publication may be reproduced or transmitted in any form
or by any means, electronic or mechanical, including photocopying, recording, or any
information storage and retrieval system, without permission in writing from the publisher.

House of Anansi Press is committed to protecting our natural environment.
As part of our efforts, the interior of this book is printed on paper that contains
at least 30% post-consumer waste recycled fibres and is processed chlorine-free.

23 22 21 20 19   1 2 3 4 5

Library and Archives Canada Cataloguing in Publication

Cataloguing data available from Library and Archives Canada

Library of Congress Control Number: 2018940911

Cover design: Chloé Griffin and Kyra Griffin
Cover artwork: Chloé Griffin
Inside cover photographs: Antonia LaMantia
Typesetting: Laura Brady

Canada Council   Conseil des Arts
for the Arts   du Canada

ONTARIO ARTS COUNCIL
CONSEIL DES ARTS DE L'ONTARIO
an Ontario government agency
un organisme du gouvernement de l'Ontario

*We acknowledge for their financial support of our publishing program the Canada Council
for the Arts, the Ontario Arts Council, and the Government of Canada.*

Printed and bound in Canada

THE
GRIFFIN
POETRY
PRIZE
Anthology 2019

A SELECTION OF THE SHORTLIST

Edited by KIM MALTMAN

ANANSI

2001

International
Yehuda Amichai
  Translated by Chana Bloch and
  Chana Kronfeld
Paul Celan
  Translated by Nikolai Popov
  and Heather McHugh
Fanny Howe
Les Murray

Canadian
Anne Carson
Ghandl of the Qayahl Llaanas
  Translated by Robert
  Bringhurst
Don McKay

2002

International
Victor Hernández Cruz
Christopher Logue
Les Murray
Alice Notley

Canadian
Christian Bök
Eirin Moure
Karen Solie

2003

International
Kathleen Jamie
Paul Muldoon
Gerald Stern
C. D. Wright

Canadian
Margaret Avison
Dionne Brand
P.K. Page

2004

International
Suji Kwock Kim
David Kirby
August Kleinzahler
Louis Simpson

Canadian
Di Brandt
Leslie Greentree
Anne Simpson

2005

International
Fanny Howe
Michael Symmons Roberts
Matthew Rohrer
Charles Simic

Canadian
Roo Borson
George Bowering
Don McKay

2006

International
Kamau Brathwaite
Durs Grünbein
Translated by Michael
Hofmann
Michael Palmer
Dunya Mikhail
Translated by Elizabeth
Winslow

Canadian
Phil Hall
Sylvia Legris
Erín Moure

2007

International
Paul Farley
Rodney Jones
Frederick Seidel
Charles Wright

Canadian
Ken Babstock
Don McKay
Priscila Uppal

2008

International
John Ashbery
Elaine Equi
César Vallejo
Translated by Clayton
Eshleman
David Harsent

Canadian
Robin Blaser
Nicole Brossard
Translated by Robert Majzels
and Erín Moure
David W. McFadden

2009

International
Mick Imlah
Derek Mahon
C. D. Wright
Dean Young

Canadian
Kevin Connolly
Jeramy Dodds
A. F. Moritz

2010

International
John Glenday
Louise Glück
Eiléan Ní Chuilleanáin
Valérie Rouzeau
    Translated by Susan Wicks

Canadian
Kate Hall
P. K. Page
Karen Solie

2011

International
Seamus Heaney
Adonis
    Translated by Khaled Mattawa
François Jacqmin
    Translated by Philip Mosley
Gjertrud Schnackenberg

Canadian
Dionne Brand
Suzanne Buffam
John Steffler

2012

International
David Harsent
Yusef Komunyakaa
Sean O'Brien
Tadeusz Różewicz
    Translated by Joanna Trzeciak

Canadian
Ken Babstock
Phil Hall
Jan Zwicky

2013

International
Ghassan Zaqtan
    Translated by Fady Joudah
Jennifer Maiden
Alan Shapiro
Brenda Shaughnessy

Canadian
David W. McFadden
James Pollock
Ian Williams

2014

International
Rachael Boast
Brenda Hillman
Carl Phillips
Tomasz Różycki
    Translated by Mira Rosenthal

Canadian
Anne Carson
Sue Goyette
Anne Michaels

2015

International	Canadian

Wang Xiaoni
    Translated by Eleanor
    Goodman
Wioletta Greg
    Translated by Marek
    Kazmierski
Michael Longley
Spencer Reece
	Shane Book
	Jane Munro
	Russell Thornton

2016

International	Canadian

Norman Dubie
Joy Harjo
Don Paterson
Rowan Ricardo Phillips
	Ulrikka S. Gernes
	    Translated by Per Brask and
	    Patrick Friesen
	Liz Howard
	Soraya Peerbaye

2017

International	Canadian

Jane Mead
Abdellatif Laâbi
    Translated by Donald
    Nicholson-Smith
Alice Oswald
Denise Riley
	Jordan Abel
	Hoa Nguyen
	Sandra Ridley

2018

International	Canadian
Tongo Eisen-Martin **Susan Howe** Layli Long Soldier Natalie Shapero	**Billy-Ray Belcourt** Aisha Sasha John Donato Mancini

CONTENTS

PREFACE

At the end of July, having just returned from Australia, I began to experience the deluge reported by Griffin judges from previous years. Every few weeks a new banker's box or two of poetry would arrive at the door, and a new round of reading and engagement would begin. Five-hundred-plus books and much reading and rereading later, my fellow judges and I began our no-longer-solitary deliberations. This took several marathon conference calls, in which we engaged in amazingly detailed discussions — of the poetry before us, and poetry more generally — that were variously challenging, illuminating, exhausting, and exhilarating. We advocated, mourned, listened; re-advocated; re-listened; mourned some more, and, in the end, all longing, I imagine, for an alternate reality with a larger number of finalist places, had to bid a complicated farewell to books we'd hoped, but had finally been unable, to take forward. Along the way, I think we all had our tastes challenged, schooled, and stretched — by the process itself, as well as by the choices, arguments, and advocacy of our fellow judges.

It goes without saying that, just as I've found personal favourites absent from previous years' shortlists (books by Lynn Crosbie and George Amabile, for example, or, going back somewhat farther, Alice Oswald's *Memorial*) so there will be those who find their own favourites absent from ours.

Poetry, however, is not (at least to most of those serious about the reading and writing of it) a competitive sport, and to focus overmuch on the winners or shortlists from any given year would be to miss the larger purpose of the prize, which is to shine a light on poetry more generally. Any jury (and ours is no exception) can be expected to represent a range of tastes, enthusiasms, and inclinations. But even so, that range is bound to be limited, and, even within that range, there were certainly more books worthy of serious consideration in 2018 than there were spaces to accommodate them. A different jury might well have come up with lists differing radically from ours. Ours should thus be viewed not so much as an attempt to identify, in any absolute sense, the three best Canadian and four best international books published in the past year, as the outcome of a process in which the three of us, collectively, took up the opportunity presented by those seven available slots to highlight seven books with what seemed to us particularly singular and compelling voices from amongst the considerably larger number of excellent books published in English in 2018. The poems that follow in this anthology should be viewed similarly, as samples — meant to give a sense of the strengths and range of each of the books represented, chosen to whet your (the reader's) appetite, and encourage you to read, engage with (and buy!), not just the seven shortlisted books, but poetry more generally.

Thanks to my fellow judges, Ulrikka Gernes and Chicu Reddy, for the pleasure of the last few months' debate, commitment, and engagement over the reading and writing of poetry, and to the inimitable Ruth Smith for keeping the whole enterprise running so smoothly.

In closing, I'd like to add to what's been said by judges going back to 2000, and express my appreciation to Scott Griffin, and the Griffin trustees, for the whole extended Griffin poetry initiative. Over the years it's managed to erect several exceptionally sturdy poles up which the flags of poetry are now routinely run, and those of us who already love poetry, as well as those yet to be fully captured and drawn permanently into its orbit, are all the better for it.

Kim Maltman, Toronto, March 2019

THE GRIFFIN POETRY PRIZE
Anthology 2019

INTERNATIONAL
SHORTLIST

RAYMOND ANTROBUS

The Perseverance

"The truth is I'm not / a fist fighter," writes Raymond Antrobus, "I'm all heart, no technique." Readers who fall for this streetwise feint may miss out on the subtle technique — from the pantoum and sestina to dramatic monologue and erasure — of *The Perseverance*. But this literary debut *is* all heart, too. Heart *plus* technique. All delivered in a voice that resists oversimple categorization. As a poet of d/Deaf experience, Antrobus writes verse that gestures toward a world beyond sound. As a Jamaican/British poet, he deconstructs the racialized empire of signs from within. Perhaps that slash between verses and signs is where the truth is.

Happy Birthday Moon

Dad reads aloud. I follow his finger across the page.
Sometimes his finger moves past words, tracing white space.
He makes the Moon say something new every night
to his deaf son who slurs his speech.

Sometimes his finger moves past words, tracing white space.
Tonight he gives the Moon my name, but I can't say it,
his deaf son who slurs his speech.
Dad taps the page, says, *try again.*

Tonight he gives the Moon my name, but I can't say it.
I say *Rain-nan Akabok.* He laughs.
Dad taps the page, says, *try again,*
but I like making him laugh. I say my mistake again.

I say *Rain-nan Akabok.* He laughs,
says, *Raymond you're something else.*
I like making him laugh. I say my mistake again.
Rain-nan Akabok. What else will help us?

He says, *Raymond you're something else.*
I'd like to be the Moon, the bear, even the rain.
Rain-nan Akabok, what else will help us
hear each other, really hear each other?

I'd like to be the Moon, the bear, even the rain.
Dad makes the Moon say something new every night
and we hear each other, really hear each other.
As Dad reads aloud, I follow his finger across the page.

Jamaican British

after Aaron Samuels

Some people would deny that I'm Jamaican British.
Anglo nose. Hair straight. No way I can be Jamaican British.

They think I say I'm black when I say Jamaican British
but the English boys at school made me choose: Jamaican,
    British?

Half-caste, half mule, house slave — Jamaican British.
Light skin, straight male, privileged — Jamaican British.

Eat callaloo, plantain, jerk chicken — I'm Jamaican.
British don't know how to serve our dishes; they enslaved us.

In school I fought a boy in the lunch hall — Jamaican.
At home, told Dad, *I hate dem, all dem Jamaicans* — I'm British.

He laughed, said, *you cannot love sugar and hate your sweetness*,
took me straight to Jamaica — passport: British.

Cousins in Kingston called me Jah-English,
proud to have someone in their family — British.

Plantation lineage, World War service, how do I serve
    Jamaican British?
When knowing how to war is Jamaican British.

The Perseverance

'Love is the man overstanding'
PETER TOSH

I wait outside THE PERSEVERANCE.
Just popping in here a minute.
I'd heard him say it many times before
like all kids with a drinking father,
watch him disappear
into smoke and laughter.

There is no such thing as too much laughter,
my father says, drinking in THE PERSEVERANCE
until everything disappears —
I'm outside counting minutes,
waiting for the man, my *father*
to finish his shot and take me home before

it gets dark. We've been here before,
no such thing as too much laughter
unless you're my mother without my father,
working weekends while THE PERSEVERANCE
spits him out for a minute.
He gives me 50p to make me disappear.

50p in my hand, I disappear
like a coin in a parking meter before
the time runs out. How many minutes
will I lose listening to the laughter
spilling from THE PERSEVERANCE
while strangers ask, *where is your father?*

I stare at the doors and say, *my father
is working*. Strangers who don't disappear
but hug me for my perseverance.
Dad said *this will be the last time* before,
while the TV spilled canned laughter,
us, on the sofa in his council flat, knowing any minute

the yams will boil, any minute,
I will eat again with my father,
who cooks and serves laughter
good as any Jamaican who disappeared
from the Island I tasted before
overstanding our heat and perseverance.

I still hear *popping in for a minute*, see him disappear.
We lose our fathers before we know it.
I am still outside THE PERSEVERANCE, listening for the laughter.

Doctor Marigold Re-evaluated

'If a written word can stand for an idea as well as a spoken word can, the same may be said of a signed word'
HARLAN LANE

My BSL teacher taught me about affirmation and negation, saying, in sign: *if you are crying and someone asks, "are you crying?" you must answer with a smile and nod to affirm, "yes, crying."*

I thought about Charles Dickens. About everyone laughing and crying in 1843 while he performed Doctor Marigold. The story is of a Cheap Jack trader pushing his cart through east London, who adopts a deaf girl called Sophy after losing his own daughter, because grief never leaves, it just changes shape. Dickens visited deaf schools, interviewed the students before shaping his story.

So let's love that Sophy and Doctor Marigold invent their own home signs. Let's love that Sophy goes to a deaf school, learns to read. Let's laugh when two deaf people fall in love.

Let's laugh when Sophy writes a letter to Doctor Marigold *hoping the child is not born deaf.* Let's laugh at the people who hope their child is born with a *pretty voice.* Let's speak in the BSL word order — *sign you speak?* — while celebrating and rolling our eyes at the signature *sentimental ending.* It's said that as Dickens read in Whitechapel, hearing people cried in the street when Sophy spoke (an unexplained miracle).

I want my BSL teacher to sign to everyone in 1843, *are you crying?* I want everyone to smile and nod, *yes, crying.*

To Sweeten Bitter

My father had four children
and three sugars in his coffee
and every birthday he bought me
a dictionary which got thicker
and thicker and because his word
is not dead I carry it like sugar

on a silver spoon
up the Mobay hills in Jamaica
past the flaked white walls
of plantation houses
past canefields and coconut trees
past the new crystal sugar factories.

I ask dictionary why we came here —
it said *nourish* so I sat with my aunt
on her balcony at the top
of Barnet Heights
and ate salt fish
and sweet potato

and watched women
leading their children
home from school.
As I ate I asked dictionary
what is difficult about love?
It opened on the word *grasp*

and I looked at my hand
holding this ivory knife
and thought about how hard it was
to accept my father
for who he was
and where he came from

how easy it is now to spill
sugar on the table before
it is poured into my cup.

Maybe I Could Love a Man

I think to myself,
sitting with cousin Shaun in the Spanish Hotel

eating red snapper and rice and peas as Shaun says,
you talk about your father a lot, but I wasn't

talking about my father, I was talking about the host
on Smile Jamaica who said to me on live TV,

if you've never lived in Jamaica you're not Jamaican.
I said, *my father born here, he brought me back every year*

wanting to keep something of his home in me,
and the host sneered. I imagine my father laughing

at all the TVs in heaven. He knew this kind of question,
being gone ten years; people said, *you from foreign now.*

Cousin Shaun lifts his glass of rum, says, *why does anyone*
try to change who their fathers are. Later, it is enough

for me to sit with Uncle Barry as he tells me in bravado
about the windows he bricked, thrown out of pubs

for standing ground against the National Front. His name
for my father was 'Bruck,' *because man always ready*

to bruck up tings, but I know my Uncle is just trying
to say, *I miss him.* Look what toughness does

to the men we love, me and Shaun are both trying to hold them.
But if our fathers could see us, sitting

in this hotel, they would laugh, not knowing
what else to do. But I walk away knowing

there are people here that remember my father,
people here who know who I am, who say

our grandfathers used to sit on that hill
and slaughter goats, while our fathers held

babies and their drinks, waving goodbye
to the people on Birch Hill who are and are not us.

DANIEL BORZUTZKY

Lake Michigan

Daniel Borzutzky's *Lake Michigan* is an elegant and chilling masterpiece of dramatic speech in a tradition of activist, political poetry that encompasses works as diverse as Pablo Neruda's *Canto General* and Peter Dale Scott's *Coming to Jakarta: A Poem about Terror*. One of the theses embodied in its multiplicity of voices might be said to be that state-sponsored (or state-acquiescent) violence creates ghosts — ghosts who, by continued speaking, come to stand in for the people from whose histories they have been created, people who are therefore never truly dead. Technically brilliant in its use of repetition and variation, leavened with touches of embittered, and yet, in the end, resilient, drollness, *Lake Michigan* is an eloquent book-length howl, a piece of political theatre staged in a no man's land lying somewhere between the surreal and the real.

Lake Michigan, Scene 1

They beat me even though I did nothing

I don't know what day it was

But they beat me on the beach

They beat me with iron paws

The mayor ordered the police superintendent to beat me

The police superintendent ordered an officer to beat me

The officer ordered his dogs to attack me

Then someone beat me with iron paws

Then someone kicked me with iron boots

Then someone shot me

Then someone buried me in the sand

Then someone scooped me out of the sand and dumped me
somewhere

And I was dead

But I could feel the sand on my body

I could feel the sand filling my mouth

I could feel the sand in my eyes

There was an earthquake in my eyes

There was a tornado in my mouth

But after the storms passed it was peaceful and I was dead

And they beat me even though I did nothing

They said I was illegal

They said I was an immigrant

They said I was an illegal immigrant who roamed the streets in a gang

They said I raped people

They said I killed people

They said I smuggled drugs in my gastrointestinal tract

They said I didn't speak the right language

They said my boss exploited me and I tried to kill him

They said my boss treated me well and I tried to kill him

They said my heart was dark

They said I peddled in blood

They said this is only war and that I had the audacity to think my body could resist the state

Let death come quickly   I asked

Let death be easy

But I did not know how long it would take

I did not know I would be under the sand forever

I did not know that in Chicago the bodies do not die when they have been strangled or riddled with bullets

A journalist asked the mayor why they killed us

I am not responsible   said the mayor

There will be an inquest   said the mayor

We will bring the perpetrators to justice   said the mayor

He was wearing a slim fitting suit and he looked handsome as the hurricane entered his mouth

He was wearing a slim fitting suit and he looked handsome as he pretended he did not live in a city of state-killed cadavers

He had gel in his hair and his shoes were nicely polished

I died and I died again and a voice said something about hope

Another voice said you pay a big price for hope

I dragged myself around the sand and I tried to make it to the water because I thought the water might carry me away but each time I took a step closer to the water the water moved farther from my body and there were faces in the water and they were calling to me and I was trying to get to them

It's what you do when you are dead

But every time I took a step toward the water the water drew
farther away

And the faces in the water were murmuring and their murmurs
grew louder and louder as I moved nearer and farther

And it is only war   a voice said   by way of explanation   as
he photographed my dead body on the sand

And I was dead though I was still breathing when I finally made
it to the water

And in the water there was another war going on in the waves

It was only the beginning of the war that would kill me again
and again

Lake Michigan, Scene 3

The bodies are on the beach

And the bodies keep breaking

And the fight is over

But the bodies aren't dead

And the mayor keeps saying   I will bring back the bodies

I will bring back the bodies that were broken

The broken bodies speak slowly

They walk slowly onto a beach that hangs over a fire

Into a fire that hangs over a city

Into a city of immigrants   of refugees   of dozens of illegal
languages

Into a city where every body is a border between one empire and
another

I don't know the name of the police officer who beats me

I don't know the name of the superintendent who orders the
police officer to beat me

I don't know the name of the diplomat who exchanged my body
for oil

I don't know the name of the governor who exchanged my body
for chemicals

The international observers tell me I'm mythological

They tell me my history has been wiped out by history

They look for the barracks but all they see is the lake and its grandeur   the flowering gardens   the flourishing beach

The international observers ask me if I remember the bomb that was dropped on my village

They ask me if I remember the torches   the camps   the ruins

They ask me if I remember the river   the birds   the ghosts

They say   find hope in hopefulness   find life in deathlessness

Locate the proper balance between living and grieving

I walk on the lake and hear voices

I hear voices in the sand and wind

I hear guilt and shame in the waves

I have my body when others are missing

I have my hands when others are severed

I hear the children of Chicago singing   *We live in the blankest of times*

Lake Michigan, Scene 6

The golden sand of Lake Michigan was here

The chromium spilled from the US Steel plant in Portage, Indiana was here

The raw sewage was here

The animal waste was here

The waters that in the sunlight reminded Simone de Beauvoir of silk and flashing diamonds were here

The seagulls were here

The liquid manure was here

The birds colonized by E. coli were here

The police removing the homeless bodies on the beach were here

The police removing the illegal immigrants on the beach were here

The police beating the mad bodies on the beach were here

The public hospitals were not here and the police had nowhere to take the sick ones to so they kicked them in the face   handcuffed them and took them to jail

A woman screamed and the external police review board heard nothing

No one heard the woman screaming and no one saw the children vomiting

No vomiting children   wrote the external review board   no
dead or decaying animals

The members of the external police review board belong to the
Democratic Party and they love to play with their children on
the beach

They belong to the ACLU and they love to play with their pets
on the beach

They volunteer at their kids' schools and they don't believe in the
bones of the disappeared

The pigs colonized by E. coli were here

The cattle colonized by E. coli were here

The humans colonized by E. coli were here

The police were here and they murdered two boys and the
external police review board saw nothing

Lake Michigan, Scene 18

The beaches are filled with cages

And the cages are filled with bodies

And the bodies are filled with burdens

And the burdens consume the bodies

And the bodies do not know to whom they owe their life

I drop my body on the sand and someone tells me to pick it up

I drop to the sand to pick up my body and someone tells me to steal more hair   to steal more flesh   to steal more bones   to steal more fingers

I tell them I cannot risk contaminating the data

I tell them that if I steal more hair then the data will not be clean

I tell them I cannot touch my own body out of fear of contaminating the data

I have a virus   I say

I am contagious   I say

No salt in my body   I say   no heat in my blood

The sand is dying slowly

It turns into a wall and in the wall there is a nook and in the nook there is light and in light there is god and in god there is nothing and in nothing there is hope and in hope there is abandonment and in abandonment there is wound and in wound there is nation and in nation there are bones and in bones there is time and in time there is light and in light there are numbers and in numbers there are codes and in codes there are mountains and in mountains there are bodies searching for bones and in the mountains there are tunnels and in the tunnels there is so much festering garbage

The men in uniform take the garbage away but they have a hard time distinguishing the garbage from the people so they scoop it all up and carry us into the next morning

And in the next morning there is a confession

I have put my burdens in the wrong body

I have framed my burdens in the wrong language

I have staked my burdens to the wrong nation

I need medicine to sleep

I need medicine to stop the shrieking in my ears

I need medicine to make the Chicago corpses turn into hydrangeas

I need medicine to make the immigrants turn into butterflies

I need an injection to make the bureaucrats turn into terrorists

It is raining again on Lake Michigan

Some say it is raining bodies   but really it is raining trash

The trash they bomb us with explodes when it lands near our bodies

And our bodies are tornadoes

And the joke turns into a mystery novel about how god keeps his hands from shaking when he is about to destroy the universe

I need my burdens   sing the bodies on the beach

I fight for my burdens   scream the bodies on the beach

I know the blankness of my burdens is a battle for love and country

I know the blankness of my burdens is a coda to the death of the city

I don't know why I can't see the moon anymore

I can't see the stars or the sky anymore

I don't even bother to look up

DON MEE CHOI

TRANSLATED FROM THE KOREAN WRITTEN BY KIM HYESOON

Autobiography of Death

In the grievous wake of the Sewol ferry incident of 2014, the Korean poet Kim Hyesoon composed a cycle of forty-nine poems — one for each day the dead must await reincarnation — to produce a harrowing work of shock, outrage, and veneration for the children lost to this disaster. Through Don Mee Choi's extraordinary translations, we hear the clamorous registers of Kim Hyesoon's art — a transnational collision of shamanism, Modernism, and feminism — yield "a low note no one has ever sung before." That otherworldly tone may sound like life itself, the poet sings, "for even death can't enter this deep inside me."

Commute

On the subway your eyes roll up once. That's eternity.

The rolled-up eyes eternally magnified.

You must have bounced out of the train. It seems that you're
    dying.

Even though you're dying, you think. Even though you're dying,
    you listen.

Oh what's wrong with this woman? People. Passing by.
You're a piece of discarded trash. Garbage to be ignored.

As soon as the train leaves, an old man comes over.
He discreetly inserts black fingernails inside your pants.

A moment later he steals your handbag.
Two middle schoolers come over. They rummage around in your
    pockets.
They kick. Camera shutters click.
Your funeral photo is on the boys' cell phones.

You watch the panorama unfold in front of you like the dead
    normally do.
Your gaze directed outward now departs for the vast space inside
    you.

Death is something that storms in from the outside. The
    universe inside is bigger.
It's deep. Soon you float up inside it.

She's stretched out over there. Like a pair of discarded pants.
When you pull up the left leg, the right leg of your pants runs

faraway, your unsewn clothes, your zipperless clothes swirl around. At the corner of the subway of your morning commute.

Pitiful. At one point the woman was embraced as bones clasp marrow,
embraced as bra cups breasts.

Black hair, coming and going, clutches. Your single outfit.

A dinosaur is about to come out of the woman's body.
She opens her eyes wide. But there's no exit left.

The woman's dead. Turned off like the night sun.
Now the woman's spoon can be discarded.
Now the woman's shadow can be folded.
Now the woman's shoes can be removed.

You run away from yourself. Like a bird far from its shadow.
You decide to escape the misfortune of living with that woman.

You shout, I don't have any feeling whatsoever for that woman!
But you roll your eyes the way the woman did when she was alive
and continue on your way to work as before. You go without your body.

Will I get to work on time? You head toward the life you won't be living.

After You're Gone
DAY SIX

After you've gone don't go, don't
After you've come don't come, don't

When you depart, they close your eyes, put your hands together
and cry don't go, don't go .
But when you say open the door, open the door, they say don't
come, don't come

They glue a paper doll onto a bamboo stick and say don't come,
don't come
They throw your clothes into the fire and say don't come, don't
come

That's why you're footless
wingless

yet all you do is fly
unable to land

You're visible even when you hide
You know everything even without a brain

You feel so cold
even without a body

That's why this morning the nightgown hiding under the bed
is sobbing quietly to itself

Water collects in your coffin
You've already left the coffin

Your head's imprint on the moon pillow
Your body's imprint on the cloud blanket

So after you've gone don't go, don't
So after you've come don't come, don't

Everyday Everyday Everyday
DAY NINE

You're holding the receiver but you're not here
You're wearing your earbuds but you're not here

The dead girl talks into a toy phone
Can I speak to my mommy? I want to sing a song for her

You're eating but you're not at the table
where maggots feast on my descendants' abdomens

The call's not going through right now but it should be alright by
    Sunday night
Will it really be okay by Saturday morning after Sunday night?

You're here but not here
You're there but not there

What if I get a tattoo on my face?
Then will I be here?

Please give me the there
the arrival after arrival

The lonely child without a phone
The girl's face is as big as the sky, the dark cloud

Like when the boats tickle the inside of your garment
Like when you talk into the mic and confess your love

Like fog, like smoke, the there tomorrow
Here is not the place, now is not the time

Sunlight tickles the heap of trash floating down the river
The tomorrow that escaped from your body turns around to look
     at you

The there is not there but here
Mommy makes money and will come tomorrow, comes every,
     every tomorrow

The faces of people holding their phones like mirrors inside the
     packed subway
are already there like the evaporated dew drops in the morning

The phone rings there
Your tongue is already there, flapping about like a tropical fish
     on the mist-soaked asphalt

Winter's Smile
DAY NINETEEN

It's cold, for you've come out from a warm body
It's bright, for you've come out from a dark body
It's lonely, for you've lost your shadow

Icy, like soil dug out from a flower pot
Sunny, like the sunlight fish stare at beneath the sheet of ice
Hot, like when lips touch a frozen door knob
Cold again, a bulb-like heart is half frozen

Cold again, as if zero is divided by zero
                    a glass divided by glass

It's alright, alright
for you're already dead

The place where you've shed yourself, the cold arrived, drained of
    all the red from your body

I Want to Go to the Island
DAY TWENTY

You leave for the island in the middle of the night.
You get on the ferry, dragging along a small bag.
It's midnight and you're bored. You can't fall asleep.
You go out on the deck. The vast sky and ocean are a black
mirror. It wavers.
You think about the sleeping fish inside the black mirror.
You think about the gluttony of the vast mirror that leaves
nothing behind, not even a single shadow.
You ponder, What if starting tomorrow the days without sunrise
continue?
Then we'd be inside this black mirror 24 hours a day, and who'd
dip a pen into the mirrorwater to write about us?
Why is there so much ink for writing?
You head to the cafeteria to shake off your ominous thoughts.
You might have heard the ship floating on black water sobbing
sadly.
You receive a phone call after midnight.
The call's about the emptiness of your being gone.
This is the thousandth call.
But emptiness over there is transmitted to you in spite of the
calls.
You go into the hallway and pick up the receiver and sing the
oldest song you know into it.
You set a time for your song to be sent.
So someone feeling empty can hear the song as soon as she
opens her eyes the next morning.
But you doze off as if you're stepping into the mirrorwater, as
you listen to the sounds the sleeping bodies make.
For the thousandth time the same seat, same posture, same
bodies, same smell, same room.
An emptiness walks into the mirrorwater. She's weeping,
caressing, and calling your name.

The light from the lighthouse dims and you awake from your
  sleep.
Because you heard the announcement for breakfast.
It's your morning call.
The same menu, same table, same radish kimchi, same taste,
  same sound, same feeling.
You look out the window. Bright sea. Clear sky. You're relieved.
You're almost there.
The sun is high up in the sky and the sea is calm. Wash your
  face, pack your bags, then it's time to disembark.
And darkness.
For the thousandth time you don't reach the island.
You won't be able to reach the island anytime soon.
The moment you think that arrival is near
you board the ferry in the middle of the night, dragging along a
  small bag.
The sound of the horn from the departing boat makes your heart
  tremor
Again, it's midnight and you're bored. You can't fall asleep.
You go out on the deck.
The vast sky and ocean are a black mirror.

Underworld

The dead without faces

run out like patients

when the door of the intensive care unit opens

carrying pouches of heart, pouches of urine

The dead running toward the path to the underworld

turn into stone pillars when they look back and their eyes meet
their past

The dead in their sacks look out with eyes brimming with salt
water

The dead become pillars of water as their tears melt their bones
The dead, gone forever, departed before you,
pull amniotic sacs over their heads and get in line to be born
again
and say that they need to learn their mother tongue all over
again
You're not there when they awake or even when they eat
breakfast
When the dead swarm down the mountain
like children who pour out of the door of the first-grade room
carrying their notebooks and shoe bags

a four-ton bronze bell with a thousand names of the dead
engraved on it dangles from the helicopter
The helicopter flies over a tall mountain to hang the bell at a
temple hidden deep in the mountains

Don't

The warm buoyant breaths don't miss you
The winds that have left for reincarnation before you, that brush
    against the lips of your childhood don't miss you

The winter, the woman's ice-heart, dead from sickness, drifting
    away in the infinite blue sky
with thin needles stuck all over it doesn't miss you

The leaves blow away, leaving their prints on the frozen river and

the one-hundred, two-hundred-storey high buildings crumble
    all at once and

the spectacles with spectacles, shoes with shoes, lips with lips,
    eyebrows with eyebrows, footprints with footprints swept
    into a huge drawer don't miss you

The river is frozen eighty centimeters deep, a tank passes over it,
    and the fish beneath the ice don't miss you

The dog tied to the electric pole in front of the tobacco shop for
    fourteen years doesn't miss you

While the big wind takes away thousands of women dead from
    madness

the sound of the "you's" of your whole life, your hair falling

all of the winter landscape, wailing and wielding its whip doesn't
    miss you

Thousands, hundreds of thousands, millions of snow flurries
    don't miss you

Don't descend all over the world, howling, murmuring,
searching for your snowman-like body buried in the snow,
don't miss you and say love you or whatever as if unfolding a
beautifully folded letter

Don't miss you just because you're not you and I'm the one who's
really you

Don't miss you as you write and write for forty-nine days with
an inkless pen

ANI GJIKA

TRANSLATED FROM THE ALBANIAN WRITTEN BY LULJETA LLESHANAKU

Negative Space

The less widely known the original language, the more precious the gift of translation! Luljeta Lleshanaku's *Negative Space* offers a rare glimpse into contemporary Albanian poetry. Effortlessly and with crisp precision, Ani Gjika, herself a poet, has rendered into English, not only the poems in *Negative Space*, but also the eerie ambience which resonates throughout the book, the deep sense of impermanence that is one of the many consequences of growing up under severe political oppression. "Negative space is always fertile." Opening trauma's door, we're met by a tender and intelligent voice with stories illuminating existence in a shared humanity, thus restoring dignity. In a world fractured by terror and violence, Lleshanaku's poetry is infinitely exciting, soothing us, its citizens.

Almost Yesterday

Strangers are building a new house next door.
They shout, swear, cheer.
Hammers and a bustle of arms.
They whistle melodies
bookended by hiccups.

Their large window opens to the east.
A lazy boy in sandals
drags a bucket of water half his size.
Sedative.
The world holds its breath for one moment.
The page turns.

Trucks loaded with cement
leave the symbol for infinity in the dirt.

Along the wall, a plumb line measures the height
like a medallion hanging into space
or from someone's neck whose face
nobody bothers to look at.

They started with the barn.
This is how a new life begins —
with an axiom.

I remember my father
returning sweaty from the fields
at lunch break; he and mother
coming out of the barn
tidying their tangled hair in a hurry,
both flushed, looking around in fear
like two thieves.

Their bedroom was cool and clean
on the first floor of the house.

I still ask myself: 'Why in the barn?'
But I also remember
that the harvest was short that year,
the livestock hungry;
we were on a budget
and switched the lights off early.

I was twelve.
My sleep deep, my curiosity numbed,
tossed carelessly to the side
like mounds of snow along the road.

But I remember the barn clearly, as if it were yesterday,
almost yesterday.
You cannot easily forget what you watch with one eye closed,
the death of the hero in the film,
or your first eclipse of the sun.

History Class

The desks in the front row were always empty.
I never understood why.
The second row was all smacking lips
of those who recited the lessons by heart.

In the middle were the timid ones
who took notes and stole the occasional piece of chalk.
And in the last row, young boys craning their heads
towards the beauty marks on the blonde girls' necks.

I don't remember the teacher's name, the room,
or the names of the portraits on the wall,
except the irony clinging to the stump of his arm
like foam around the Cape of Good Hope.

When his healthy arm pointed out Bismarck,
his hollow sleeve gestured in an unknown direction.
We couldn't tell which one of us was the target,
making us question
the tiniest bit of who we thought we were.

Out of his insatiable mouth flew battle dates,
names, causes. Never resolutions or winners.
We could hardly wait for the bell
to write our own history,
as we already knew everything in those days.

But sometimes his hollow sleeve
felt warm and human, like a cricket-filled summer night.
It hovered, waiting to land somewhere. On a valley or roof.
It searched for a hero among us —
not among the athletic or sparkly-eyed ones,
but among those stamped with innocence.

One day, each one of us will be that teacher
standing before a seventeen-year-old boy
or a girl with a beauty mark on her neck.
And the desks in the front row will remain empty,
abandoned by those who are always in doubt.
They're the missing arm of history
that makes the other arm appear omnipotent.

January 1, Dawn

After the celebrations,
people, TV channels, telephones,
the year's recently corrected digit
finally fall asleep.

Between the final night and the first dawn
a jagged piece of sky
as if viewed from the open mouth of a whale.
Inside her belly and inside the belly of time,
there's no point worrying.
You glide gently along. She knows her course.
Inside her, you are digested slowly, painlessly.

And if you're lucky, like Jonah,
at some point she'll spit you out on dry land
along with heaps of inorganic waste.

Everything sleeps. A sweet hypothermic sleep.
But those few still awake
might hear the melancholy creaking of a wheelbarrow,
someone stealing stones from a ruin
to build new walls just a few feet away.

Fishermen's Village

Squinty, salt-dusted windows face the distance.
They all look seaward.

Every third person here has the same name:
perhaps the name of a godparent
who cut her first lock of hair
before the wind thickened it,
or a stranger's name . . .
The locals, by the way, welcome the strangers,
because they were told
that one of them who once walked barefoot on water
used to load the sardine boats
with swift hands.

Foreigners are easily identified;
unlike the locals, their clothes are white, blue, jet black.
And sometimes,
they make you a gift of rosaries or cigars.
Once, one of them
left a pair of shoes behind
and the whole village gathered to play the lottery.
When someone with an already good pair of shoes won,
the young men who had been keenly following the show,
kicked the sand in anger,
'What the hell? It's not fair!'

Sand everywhere. All day long,
overturned boats on the shore
eat sand. Night stars feed on the sand.
The boats beached here since the last war
people remember brought
Omega watches strapped

to soldiers' wrists, and herpes
that spread from flesh to flesh
faster than wind
and faster than famine.

Cats purr behind doors.
Streets reek of fish and yet there are no fish.
Noontime, a man dozes on a sofa in the yard.
His wife sits at his feet, mending
the net with needle and thread,
which she cuts with her teeth.

Eyes half-open, he gazes at her
realising here is the real cause: the large hole in the net,
a hole first torn two thousand years ago after a prosperous
    fishing night,
when things were sorted out much like they are today:
some cursed with luck and some blessed with mercy.

This Gesture

Look what we have here:
some books bought with a little savings,
as if land purchased for a house
that you might never build. Plato, Hegel, *The Marxist Movement*,
heavy cloth covers. Sideways, behind Aristotle, rests Art
    Nouveau,
like the head of a woman nodding off on the train,
your shoulder still out of politeness.
Books in foreign languages, bought with the last change
from shops you'll never visit again:
Tarkovsky's Techniques, exchanged for five food vouchers;
Bergman, Hitchcock, Luis Buñuel reveal only part of the wall,
each the end of a misleading path inside a pyramid.
African Masks, Aztec Culture, Egyptian Gods
all bought on a rainy day perhaps, as an excuse to stay indoors.
And again the visual arts albums
labelled *Ars* in Latin like medicinal bottles
that camouflage a bitter taste.

Hugo, Turgenev, Stendhal . . .
relics of first love, second love, of . . .
A dark empty space
and further, Dostoyevsky's *White Nights*
with its green irony on the cover that says,
'Throw a coat over your shoulders first . . .'

And lower, Gaudí and other architectural books . . .
A smooth transition between what you wanted
and what you were able to attain.
Encyclopaedias, temples without roofs.
Shakespeare exchanged for a noisy Soviet radio.

Poetry books: thin, sly, bought at discounted prices,
breaking apart like crumbled bread thrown at swans in the park.

The only ones arranged horizontally
are *The Erotic Art of the Middle Ages*, *The Ethical Slut*, and *Tropic of*
  Cancer —
easy to find when feeling around in the dark,
like slippers under the bed.

In a corner, the holy books, the Gospels.
They've arrived here by themselves — you didn't spend a cent to
  buy them.
Each volume almost never opened. How can you believe
  something
that doesn't ask for anything in exchange?

And on the very bottom, *The Barbarian Invasion*, history, science . . .
Time to read with glasses. Linear reading. Andropause.

To show someone your library is an intimate gesture,
like giving him a map, a tourist map of the self
marked with the museums, parks, bridges, galleries, hotels,
  churches, subway . . .
and the graveyards that appear regularly
at the edges of every town, at the beginning of every epoch.

The Stairs

My father was obsessed with stairs.
All his life he'd build one set and destroy another,
sometimes indoors, sometimes outdoors,
never finding the perfect way to go up.

I feel the same way.

There's a different view from above: streets
become tight ropes; gardens hide behind houses
like bite marks on a lover's neck; cosmic dust conceals
the rotation of pedestrians around a star and themselves.
Whereas the railroad track with its yellow and black lines
isn't the rattlesnake that makes your skin crawl . . .

Whenever I chose the quick stairs of the elevator,
l got stuck between floors, an irrational number.
What happened next not worth mentioning.

And then the escalators
that deliver you
intact
like a postal package to another era
without knowing what's inside you. You don't know either.

Poetry, too, is a way of moving up,
temptation through denial, *via negativa*,
but the room on the second floor stays damp and cold, vacant.

My aunt shows a scar on her knee
from her youth, caused by a nail on a wooden staircase —
she tells the same story over and over again.

I never understood what she was looking for,
those summer evenings on the roof,
but I imagine the sad creaking on the stairs, her solemn descent,
her cadence, like all other cadences, without nails, without
wounds.

CANADIAN
SHORTLIST

DIONNE BRAND

The Blue Clerk

Dionne Brand's *The Blue Clerk* is many things at once: a book-length *ars poetica*; an act of memory and reconfiguration; an extended meditation (one that moves at times directly, at others by a kind of philosophical osmosis) touching on the realms of history, politics, race, and gender; an internal, consciously curated and interrogated dialogue that manages to create a space for all of these. Expansive, beautifully written, structurally compelling, and above all moving, *The Blue Clerk* is a book to be read (and reread), not just for the pleasures of its language, but for the breadth of its vision, and the capaciousness of its thinking.

Verso 1.1.01

When Borges says he remembers his father's library in Buenos Aires, the gaslight, the shelves, and the voice of his father reciting Keats's "Ode to a Nightingale," I recall the library at the roundabout on Harris Promenade. The library near the Metro Cinema and the Woolworths store. But to go back, when my eyes lit first on Borges's dissertation I thought, I had no Library. And I thought this thought with my usual melancholy and next my usual pride in living without.

And the first image that came to me after that was my grandfather's face with his tortoiseshell spectacles and his weeping left eye and his white shirt and his dark seamed trousers and his newspaper and his moustache and his clips around his shirt sleeves and his notebooks and his logbooks; and at the same moment that the melancholy came it was quickly brushed aside by the thought that he was my library.

In his notebooks, my grandfather logged hundredweight of copra, pounds of chick feed and manure; the health of horses, the nails for their iron shoes; the acreages of coconut and tania; the nuisance of heliconia; the depth of two rivers; the length of a rainy season.

Then I returned to Harris Promenade and the white library with wide steps, but when I ask, there was no white library with wide steps, they tell me, but an ochre library at a corner with great steps leading up. What made me think it was a white library? The St. Paul's Anglican Church anchoring the lime white Promenade, the colonial white Courthouse, the grey white public hospital overlooking the sea? I borrowed a book at that white library even though the library as I imagine it now did not exist. A book by Gerald Durrell, namely, *My Family and Other Animals*. I don't remember any other books I brought home, though I remember a feeling of quiet luxury and a desire for spectacles to seem as intelligent as my grandfather.

And I read here, too, in this white library a scrap about Don Quixote and Sancho Panza, though only the kind of scrap, the kind of refuse, or onion skin, they give schoolchildren in colonial countries about a strange skinny man on a horse with a round sidekick. The clerk would say I could use this, but I can't.

The ochre library on Harris Promenade was at the spot that was called "Library Corner" and it used to be very difficult to get to because of the traffic and the narrow sidewalk. But I was agile and small. And I thought I was ascending a wide white-stepped library. And though that was long ago, I remember the square clock tower adjacent to the roundabout. And I can see the Indian cinema next door, papered with the film *Aarti* starring Meena Kumari and Ashok Kumar.

My grandfather with his logs and notebooks lived in a town by the sea. That sea was like a lucent page to the left of the office where my grandfather kept his logs and his notebooks with their accounts. Apart from the depth of the two rivers, namely the Iguana and the Pilot, he also noted the tides and the times of their rising and falling.

moonrise	*5.34 a.m.*	
high tide	*5.48 a.m.*	*0.82 ft*
sunrise	*5.56 a.m.*	
low tide	*12.40 p.m.*	*0.03 ft*
new moon	*4.45 p.m.*	
sunset	*6.23 p.m.*	
high tide	*6.33 p.m.*	*0.56 ft*
low tide	*12.02 a.m.*	*0.16 ft*

Spring tides, the greatest change between high and low. Neap tides, the least.

And, the rain, he recorded, the number of inches and its absence. He needed to know about the rain for sunning and drying the copra. And, too, he kept a log of the sun, where it would be and at what hour, and its angle to the earth in what season. And come to think of it he must have logged the clouds moving in. He said that the rain always came in from the sea. The clouds moving in were a constant worry. I remember the rain sweeping in, pelting down like stones. That is how it used to be said, the rain is pelting down like stones. He filled many logbooks with rain and its types: showers, sprinkles, deluges, slanted, boulders, pebbles, sheets, needles, slivers, pepper. Cumulonimbus clouds. Or, Nimbostratus clouds. Convection rain and relief rain. *Relief rain* he wrote in his logbook in his small office, and the rain came in from the sea like pepper, then pebbles, then boulders. It drove into his window and disturbed his logs with its winds and it wet his desk. And he or someone else would say, "But look at rain!" And someone else would say, "See what the rain do?" As if the rain were human. Or they would say, "Don't let that rain come in here." As if the rain were a creature.

Anyway, my grandfather had a full and thorough record of clouds and their seasons and their violence.

From under the sea a liquid hand would turn a liquid page each eight seconds. This page would make its way to the shore and make its way back. Sometimes pens would wash up onto the beach, long stem-like organic styli. We called them pens; what tree or plant or reef they came from we did not know. But some days the beach at Guaya would be full of these styli just as some nights the beach would be full of blue crabs. Which reminds me now of García Márquez's old man with wings but didn't then as I did not know García Márquez then and our blue crabs had nothing to do with him. It is only now that the crabs in his story have overwhelmed my memory. It is only now that my blue night crabs have overwhelmed his story. Anyway we would take these pens and sign our names, and the names of those we loved, along the length of the beach. Of course these names rubbed out quickly, and as fast as we could write them the surf consumed them. And later, much much later, I learned those pens were *Rhizophora mangle* propagules.

What does this have to do with Borges? Nothing at all. I walked into the library and it was raining rain and my grandfather's logs were there, and the wooden window was open. As soon as I opened the door, down the white steps came the deluge. If I could not read I would have drowned.

Now you are sounding like me, the clerk says. I am you, the author says.

Verso 4

To verse, to turn, to bend, to plough, a furrow, a row, to turn
around, toward, to traverse

When I was nine coming home one day from school, I
stood at the top of my street and looked down its gentle
incline, toward my house obscured by a small bend, taking
in the dipping line of the two-bedroom scheme of houses,
called Mon Repos, my rest. But there I've strayed too far
from the immediate intention. When I was nine coming
home from school one day, I stood at the top of my street
and knew, and felt, and sensed looking down the gentle
incline with the small houses and their hibiscus fences,
their rosebush fences, their ixora fences, their yellow and
pink and blue paint washes; the shoemaker on the left
upper street, the dressmaker on the lower left, and way to
the bottom the park and the deep culvert where a boy on a
bike pushed me and one of my aunts took a stick to his
mother's door. Again, when I was nine coming home one
day in my brown overall uniform with the white blouse, I
stood on the top of my street knowing, coming to know in
that instant when the sun was in its four o'clock phase and
looking down I could see open windows and doors and
front door curtains flying out. I was nine and I stood at the
top of the street for no reason except to make the descent
of the gentle incline toward my house where I lived with
everyone and everything in the world, my sisters and my
cousins were with me, we had our bookbags and our four
o'clock hunger with us and our grandmother and every-
thing we loved in the world were waiting in the yellow
washed house, there was a hibiscus hedge and a buttercup
bush and zinnias waiting and for several moments all this
seemed to drift toward the past; again when I was nine
and stood at the head of my street and looked down
the gentle incline toward my house in the four o'clock

coming-home sunlight, it came over me that I was not
going to live here all my life, that I was going away and
never returning some day. A small wind brushed every-
thing or perhaps it did not but afterward I added a small
wind because of that convention in movies, but something
like a wave of air, or a wave of time passed over the small
street or my eyes, and my heart could not believe my
observation, a small wind passed over my heart drying it
and I didn't descend the gentle incline and go home to my
house and my grandmother and tell her what had hap-
pened, I didn't enter the house that was washed with
yellow distemper that we had painted on the previous
Christmas, I didn't enter the house and tell her how
frightened I was by the thought I had at the top of our
street, the thought of never living there, which seemed as if
it meant never having existed, or never having known her,
I never told her the melancholy I felt or the intrusion the
thought represented. I never descended that gentle incline
of the street toward my house, the I who I was before that
day went another way, she disappeared and became the I
who continued on to become who I am. I do not know
what became of her, where she went, the former I who
separated once we came to the top of the street and looked
down and something like a breeze that would be added
later after watching many movies passed over us. What
became of her, the one who gave in so easily or was she so
surprised to find that thought that would overwhelm her
so, and what made her keep quiet. When I was nine and
coming home one day, my street changed just as I stood at
the top of it and I knew I would never live there again or
all my life. The thought altered the afternoon and my life
and after that I was in a hurry to leave. There was another
consciousness waiting for a little girl to grow up and think
future thoughts, waiting for some years to pass and some
obligatory life to be lived until I would arrive here. When I

was nine I left myself and entered myself. It was at the top of the street, the street was called MacGillvary Street, the number was twenty-one, there were zinnias in the front yard and a buttercup bush with milky sticky pistils we used to stick on our faces. After that all the real voices around me became subdued and I was impatient and dissatisfied with everything, I was hurrying to my life and I stood outside of my life. I never arrived at my life, my life became always standing outside of my life and looking down its incline and seeing the houses as if in a daze. It was a breeze, not a wind, a kind of slowing of the air, not a breeze, a suspension of the air when I was nine standing at the top of MacGillvary Street about to say something I don't know what and turning about to run down. No, my grandmother said never to run pell-mell down the street toward the house as ill-behaved people would, so I was about to say something, to collect my cousins and sisters into an orderly file and to walk down to our hibiscus-fenced house with the yellow outer walls and my whole life inside. A small bit of air took me away.

Verso 32.2

My ancestral line to John Locke. When he wrote "An Essay Concerning Human Understanding" in 1689 he had already been the Secretary of the Board of Trade and Plantations. No one disputes this. He had, too, investments in the Royal African Company, whose holdings along the Gambia included forts, factories, and military command of West Africa, etc., . . . etc., . . . No dispute here either. These statements — an essay on human understanding, and the board of trade and plantations — these identifiers can lie beside each other with no discomfort, apparently. But as I said, I am a soft-hearted person. I cannot get past this. All and any interpretative strategies are of no help to me. I am just a lover with a lover's weaknesses, with her manifest of heartaches.

Verso 40.6

M sent me a photograph by Daguerre. It is of the first
human being to be photographed. Someone is cleaning the
shoes of someone. All descriptions of the photograph claim
that the first human being to be photographed is the figure
having his shoes cleaned. I see first the figure cleaning the
shoes as the photograph's subject. Secondly, the event of
the shoe-cleaning. From this immediately I saw the state of
the world.

Verso 55

When I finally arrived at the door of no return, there was
an official there, a guide who was a man in his ordinary life,
or a dissembler. Exhausted violet, the clerk interjects. Yes,
says the author. Violet snares. He arranged himself at the
end of the story. Violet files. Violet chemistry. Violet unction.
It was December, we had brought a bottle of rum; some
ancient ritual we remembered from nowhere and no one.
We stepped one behind the other as usual. The castle was
huge, opulent. We went like pilgrims. You were pilgrims.
We were pilgrims. This is the holiest we ever were. Our
gods were in the holding cells. We awakened our gods, and
we left them there, since we never needed gods again. We
did not have wicked gods so they understood. They lay in
their corners, on their disintegrated floors, they lay on their
walls of skin dust. They stood when we entered, happy to
see us. Our guide said, this was the prison cell for the men,
this was the prison cell for the women. I wanted to strangle
the guide. As if he were the original guide. It took all my
will. Yet in the rooms the guide was irrelevant. The gods
woke up and we felt pity for them, and affection, and love.
They felt happy for us, we were still alive. Yes, we are still
alive, we said. And we had returned to thank them. You are
still alive, they said. Yes, we are still alive. They looked at us
like violet; like violet teas they drank us. We said, here we
are. They said, you are still alive. We said, yes, yes, we are
still alive. How lemon, they said, how blue like fortune. We
took the bottle of rum from our veins, we washed their
faces, we sewed their thin skins. We were pilgrims, they
were gods. They said with wonder and admiration, you are
still alive, like hydrogen, like oxygen.

   We all stood there for some infinite time. We did weep
but that is nothing in comparison.

Verso 33.1

If I see a patch of corn, in front of a house as I did this morning, or a zinnia bed, or a wrecked mattress leaning on the side of a house, an emotion overtakes. Not one of sadness as you may imagine, you being you, but a familiarity, a grace of some weight. I might even say longing, because it occurs to me that in the zinnia, the desultory mattress, there used to be hope, not a big hope, but a tendril one for the zinnias' success, or the mattress' resurrection—the nights slept on it and the afternoons spent jumping on it. And then the scraggle of corn fighting waterless earth. A small, present happiness and an eternal hope, even also, joy.

If I see a patch of flowers near a road surviving heat and exhaust fumes and boots, a homesickness washes me and I am standing in the front yard looking at zinnias. The dire circumstances in the house behind, the material circumstances, the poverty, are part of this homesickness. Not because, one, the scarcity, and two, the zinnias, set each other off as some might think, but because they were the same.

EVE JOSEPH

Quarrels

In *Quarrels*, Eve Joseph's delightful collection of prose poems, you enter the marvellous and that is the truth! The poet has surrendered herself to the realm of the illogical, trusting that it has a logic of its own, and the outcome is, indeed, a new music. These poems are intriguing spaces and moments defeating the boundaries of the real, but rest assured, Joseph leads you by the hand with warmth, wit, and empathy.

Perhaps these poems are crystallizations of a deeply human, spiritual knowledge, gathered over decades working in a hospice. Joseph's previous book, the exceptional memoir, *In the Slender Margin*, renders this experience. Certainly, without gravity, poems wouldn't be able to sing. As distillations of life, these poems, with beauty and charm, hold their own credibility: an omnipresent, merely-in-glimpses-tangible marvellousness, miraculously fastened to the pages of a single slender volume that will fit into most pockets and assure magnificent company on any given journey.

WE MET AT A BIRTHDAY PARTY. YOU WERE THE ONLY RUM drinker in the room. On the couch, Al Purdy was going on about the stunted trees in the Arctic. Upon closer examination, we could see that the leaves were tiny parkas. The illogical must have a logic of its own you said. The first two drinks don't count, it's the third that blows the door open. With every gust of wind the little coats raised their arms and waved shyly at us. You were a new music, something I had not heard before. As they used to say about that Estonian composer: he only had to shake his sleeves and the notes would fall out.

THE RAIN HAS STOPPED AND THE SKY HAS CLEARED. MY husband is downstairs chatting with Milosz, who is chopping vegetables for dinner. I can't make out the words, only the swell of the sea and those two soldiers rowing. Milosz is wearing my apron and drinking my wine. The tide has come in, erasing the muddy footprints and the sign for *Help* carved in the sand. How do we ever return? How is it possible? I'm told a massive tree flourishes in the heart of the favela, like the pink lungs of a coal miner. He puts the oar down and caresses me with his callused hands. He knows who he is. Not the cook; the other one.

MY MOTHER WAS A WHITE SHEET DRYING ON THE LINE. Wooden clothespins held her tight as she lifted and snapped and filled like a sail. At night, when she covered me, I inhaled lily of the valley, burning leaves, the starched collar of a nurse's uniform and the stillness of a recently abandoned room. She taught me how to iron the creases out of a man's shirt after all the men had disappeared. My mother played piano by ear in the basement. A long line of hungry people gathered outside to hear her play. They wanted news from home. Overhead, handkerchiefs fluttered in the breeze. Little telegrams sent but never delivered.

YOU KNOCK ON THE DOOR BUT NOBODY ANSWERS. CUPPING your hands around your face you peer through the side-panel of frosted glass. A kettle is whistling, a woman singing as she sets the table. This is a familiar house. You knock again. Inside, the sounds are festive. Glasses clink and a band starts up. Pressing your ear to the door, you hear the sound of your own laughter. This is the house you grew up in. You're sure of it now. The revelers are boisterous, their dancing shadows on the lawn. Your legs are cold, there's frost on your shoes, and the cabby calls impatiently from the street. You remember a song that eluded you all day.

DARKNESS ARRIVES WITHOUT DRAWING ATTENTION TO itself. Porch lights flick on down the block. We're bathed in intimacy, a united front against danger—the bin diver, nasty drunk, vicious dog. The girl who works in the corner grocery store sweeps the floors and puts out mousetraps. A few dry leaves rustle in at the door when she shakes out the rug. Under fluorescent lights, she moves like an actress in a one-woman play. Night is preoccupied with arrivals and departures. The woman keeping vigil at her husband's bedside can't say if it's relief or sorrow she feels when he wakes with a shudder at dawn.

A FIVE-YEAR-OLD ASKS HIS MOTHER IF THE CLOUDS ARE
solid and wants to know why, when he looks up, he can't
see the old people and their old cats. I must have dozed
off. The trees were bare when I fell asleep but now their
leaves are that impossible newly minted green. Tom Waits
is bellowing downstairs and any second now someone I
love is going to walk through the door. I want to know
why the clouds told the Serbian poet their names in the
quiet of a summer afternoon. And why didn't he share
those names with the rest of us? Perhaps they did not
translate into English. Perhaps the old want to stay
hidden and keep their secrets all to themselves.

RIDING HOME IN THE AMBULANCE, I TUCKED MY KNEES IN tight so as not to bump the stretcher. I was studying your face. Memorizing it. Out the back window, the golden California hills receded. We swayed as if we were in a fishing boat headed to open water. When the paramedic asked, *Who's the sitting President?* you roared back to life, spitting and sputtering. Your old warring self. At Vineyard Road, the back doors opened and you were held for a brief moment between earth and sky; before the wheels hit the ground and off you went, a casualty on an improvised litter, into your own grievously listing house.

HE'LL JUST SLIP AWAY, THE NURSE SAID. AND ALL I COULD think of was a boy's mad scramble up an impossible slope. Pebbles rolling like ball bearings underfoot. She meant, I'm sure, that you'd slip out the door, unnoticed, like a sober guest when the party gets going. But all I could see was you losing your footing. Scree piled around your hospital bed, rock shards glinting at the base of the cliff. The whole mountainside unstable. On a piece of torn paper, tucked inside a book on the bedside table, a hastily written note said, *Something that was secret will emerge and something that was known will retreat into secrecy.*

THE HORSES, WHEN I FINALLY FIND THEM, IN THE DRY
hills near the reservoir, seem to be waiting for me. They
don't move or open their eyes. Like old people sleeping
in the sun, they know who's come to visit and who has
not. I was not allowed to wash or dress your corpse. Nor
light a candle in the dark house. There was no raft
pushed out to sea and nothing set on fire. The words of
the mourning prayer *yitgadal v'yitkadash sh'mei raba* were
indecipherable. This is what I've come to tell the horses.
Their ears tilt toward me. The half-circle pencil sweep of
their jawlines exactly like the ones in *The Sketchbook of
Horses*. On this dusty hill, a lone vulture circling
overhead, their long heads bow in consolation — for I
know now, that's what this is.

SARAH TOLMIE

The Art of Dying

A modern *danse macabre* in eighty-nine parts, Sarah Tolmie's *The Art of Dying* conceals a multifaceted meditation on mortality beneath its deceptively simple lyric surface. An irreverent feminist in the tradition of Dorothy Parker and Stevie Smith, Tolmie leverages the subversive possibilities of doggerel to upend our assumptions about everything from abortion to the Anthropocene. Wickedly funny, this is work of great intimacy, too, introducing us to a mother, concerned citizen, social media addict, bookworm, and bon vivant who wants nothing more than to remain "Here on the quiet earth that I still love, / Where the last humans are."

It continues fashionable to mourn the death of ritual.
We miss the Neolithic ochre, smoking censers, silly hats
Cthulhu and Harryhausen prayers, all the mystic flap.

No one has ever owned death much better than that.
Still, ours are not that bad.
Hospitals have strict norms,

Specific times and tricky forms,
Rotting fruit and flowers.
We say conventional things at canonical hours.

I had to abort a fetus once at fourteen weeks.
That sucked but was less agony
Than its putative life, all back to front, a wreck.

Such moments of naked horror let us see
The bloodyminded fervour of the selfish gene.
If you look around you, you will learn

Almost every woman that you know
Has lost a baby or two.
Lost. As if you left it on the bus

Or it just fell out of your uterus
In a Monty Python sketch.
Behind the screen of this careful word,

The old truths of the sisterhood:
Not to be judged, or feared, or harmed
Because of a child not in your arms.

39

Oliver Sacks is going to die,
He tells us blithely in the *New York Times*.
He's 81. His liver's shot.

He's blind in one eye
Though when both worked fine
He could still get lost in a parking lot.

He's extremely famous and terribly shy.
He's lost his leg but it's still attached.
He's been practicing dying, Oliver Sacks.

He will do it well,
Politely evading heaven and hell.
Doctor Oliver Sacks, farewell.

60

Death does not end co-dependence.
Isn't this what culture means—
Alive and dead in solidarity?

Yet what is it that we see
When a parent dies, and one remains?
Half a person, wandering in pain.

Culture is strong. It tells us what to do.
It bridges the great spans with rules.
Still, we fall between the stools

After the funeral.

In this, precisely, is love cruel:
It does not die at death
But borrows tools from immortality.

Tools that do not fit the hand:
Drills that gouge the walls, saws too strong to bend,
Hammers with claws that rend our houses tearing out a nail.

Would it not be better to forget
Our loved ones at their deaths?
People speak of intersubjectivity

Like it's a great thing: I am you and you are me
And so on. Then what happens when
You die, and I am left

Half-massed? A drifting ship, unballasted?
The brain's one lonely hemisphere?
When you're half gone

And I'm half here.

67

We are scared to death by the words for things.
Even yet, when we should know better.
I know my father's teeth will chatter

If I say *pneumonia* about my son.
Suddenly it is World War One
And influenza, HINI

And doom and liver flukes.
It's Bay of Pigs and waiting nukes.

And me? I am a heartless bitch
For saying he should get a grip.

My son's imaginary friend just bit the dust:
Yukio the fabulous.

He was born on a Monday, fair of face.
The first day of our island stay.

He lived eleven days,
Protean, in rocks and waves.

At night he occupied stuffed toys.
Invisible, he biked beside.

He ran a magic portal between worlds:
This one and the digital.

Sometimes he was sand in a bottle.
A constant interlocutor.

He sickened when we went away,
Like any good *genius loci*.

He was weak and flushed.
My son told him not to get up.

He tucked him into his own bed.
Soon enough Yukio was dead.

Yukio!

The funeral is later today.
There will be dirges, bacon sandwiches, homemade punch
for Yukio, who was with us once.

In memoriam Tennyson said
Nine years of things about his friend
Who'd died. He brought him back by slow
Degrees, from sunsets, wind in the trees,

Gathering pieces painstakingly.
Tennyson, in his purity;
He never lied, never missed his line.
Grief became him metrically.

It made him blind. All he could see
Was Hallam's absence: the whole world
A cancelled cheque, crumpled and furled,
Unspent inside his pocketbook.

There its yellowing edges curled
Until his friend crept out, imbued
Everything and made it new.
At second look, he saw it through

Lost eyes, and it was dearer far
Than it had been before. A borrowed
Death does that for you. Your own cannot.
We each will miss the lesson that

We've taught. Compassion is what we learn
From those who die and don't return.
Grief gives us that hitch in the eye,
Catching on things as they pass by.

Tonight the fattened mermaids sing
To issue in the internet of things.
Let me tell you what you can do with that misnomer.
I sit here gloomily and think of Homer,

On the dimming beach, as drifts of trash
Clatter softly against my ankles,
The melancholy, long, withdrawing roar
Of everything a humanist holds dear.

Skyward the sad elite have all withdrawn,
To their electric world. They've pulled it on
Over the old like a transparent plastic glove.

I hear them pinging dismally afar.
Here on the quiet earth that I still love,
Where the last humans are.

THE POETS

RAYMOND ANTROBUS was born in Hackney, London, England, to an English mother and a Jamaican father. He is the recipient of fellowships from Cave Canem, Complete Works III, and Jerwood Compton Poetry. He is one of the world's first recipients of an M.A. in Spoken Word Education from Goldsmiths, University of London. Antrobus is a founding member of Chill Pill and the Keats House Poets Forum. He has had multiple residencies in deaf and hearing schools around London, as well as Pupil Referral Units. In 2018 he was awarded the Geoffrey Dearmer Award by the Poetry Society. He lives in London, England.

DANIEL BORZUTZKY is a poet and translator, and the author of *The Performance of Becoming Human*, winner of the 2016 National Book Award for Poetry. His other books include *In the Murmurs of the Rotten Carcass Economy*, *Memories of My Overdevelopment*, and *The Book of Interfering Bodies*. His translation of Galo Ghigliotto's *Valdivia* won the 2017 National Translation Award. Other translations include Raúl Zurita's *The Country of Planks* and *Song for His Disappeared Love*, and Jaime Luis Huenún's *Port Trakl*. He lives in Chicago.

DIONNE BRAND was born in Trinidad and is a poet, novelist, nonfiction writer, filmmaker, educator, and activist. She has written ten previous books of poetry, and is a winner of the Governor General's Award, the Trillium Book Award, the Pat Lowther

Memorial Award, and a past winner of the Griffin Poetry Prize. She was Toronto's third Poet Laureate, from 2009 to 2012. In 2017 she was named to the Order of Canada. Brand is a professor in the School of English and Theatre Studies at the University of Guelph. She lives in Toronto.

DON MEE CHOI was born in Seoul, Korea, and is the author of *Hardly War* (2016), and *The Morning News Is Exciting* (2010). She has received the 2011 Whiting Award for Poetry, a Lannan Literary Fellowship, and the 2012 Lucien Stryk Translation Prize.

ANI GJIKA is an Albanian-born poet, literary translator, and writer. Her book *Bread on Running Waters* (2013) was a finalist for the 2011 Anthony Hecht Poetry Prize, and the 2011 May Sarton New Hampshire Poetry Prize. Gjika moved to the United States when she was eighteen, earning an M.A. in English at Simmons College, and an M.F.A. in poetry at Boston University. Her honours include awards and fellowships from the National Endowment for the Arts, the Robert Pinsky Global Fellowship, English PEN Translates, Framingham State University's Miriam Levine Award, and the Robert Fitzgerald Translation Prize.

KIM HYESOON, born in 1955, is one of the most prominent and influential contemporary poets of South Korea. She was the first female poet to receive the prestigious Kim Su-young and Midang awards, and has been translated into Chinese, French, German, Japanese, Spanish, and Swedish. Her most recent books include *I'm OK, I'm Pig!* (2014), and *Poor Love Machine* (2016).

EVE JOSEPH's two previous books of poetry, *The Startled Heart* (2004) and *The Secret Signature of Things* (2010), were both nominated for the Dorothy Livesay Award. Her nonfiction book, *In the Slender Margin* (2014), won the Hubert Evans Non-Fiction Prize. Joseph grew up in North Vancouver, British Columbia, and now lives in Victoria.

LULJETA LLESHANAKU was born in Elbasan, Albania. She is the author of seven books of poetry in Albanian. Book-length translations of her work into other languages include *Antipastoral* (Italy, 2006), *Kinder der Natur* (Austria, 2010), *Dzieci natury* (Poland, 2011), and *Lunes en Siete Días* (Spain, 2017). She has won several prestigious awards for her poetry, including PEN Albania 2016, and the International Kristal Vilenica Prize in 2009. In 2012 she was one of two finalists in Poland for the European Poet of Freedom Prize.

SARAH TOLMIE is an associate professor of English at the University of Waterloo. Her poetry collection *Trio* was shortlisted for the 2016 Pat Lowther Award. She is a medievalist trained at the University of Toronto and University of Cambridge.

THE JUDGES

ULRIKKA GERNES was born in Sweden of Danish parents. At the age of twenty-two she moved to Copenhagen, Denmark, already a published and highly acclaimed poet. Her first collection, *Natsvæmer*, was published in 1984. Since then she has published an additional ten collections, two books for children, and many short stories, songs, and various contributions to literary anthologies, art catalogues, magazines, newspapers, and Danish National Radio. Per Brask and Patrick Friesen's translation of her collection *Frayed Opus for Strings & Wind Instruments* was shortlisted for the 2016 Griffin Poetry Prize. She manages the estate and artistic legacy of her father, the internationally known visual artist Poul Gernes, and lives in Copenhagen, Denmark, with her daughter.

KIM MALTMAN is a poet, theoretical particle physicist, and occasional translator who has published five books of solo poetry, over two hundred papers in the scientific literature, and three books of collaborative poetry, most recently *Box Kite* (2016). In addition to recent solo work which has appeared under a variety of heteronyms, he is involved, in collaboration with Roo Borson, in ongoing translations of the Tang Dynasty poet Li Bai and Song Dynasty poet Su Shi. Past honours include the CBC Literary Prize, and, with collaborators Roo Borson and Andy Patton, the Malahat Poetry Prize, the Earle Birney Prize, and two National Magazine Award finalist appearances. Perhaps his most unusual literary credit is having served as consulting dog poetry editor for André Alexis's novel *Fifteen Dogs.*

SRIKANTH REDDY is the author of *Voyager*, which was named one of the best books of poetry in 2011 by *The New Yorker*, *The Believer*, and National Public Radio. His previous collection, *Facts for Visitors*, won the 2005 Asian American Literary Award for Poetry. A book of literary criticism, *Changing Subjects: Digressions in Modern American Poetry*, was published in 2012. The National Endowment for the Arts, the Creative Capital Foundation, and the Guggenheim Foundation have awarded him grants and fellowships, and in fall 2015, he delivered the Bagley Wright Lectures in Poetry. A graduate of the Iowa Writers' Workshop and the doctoral program in English at Harvard University, he is currently an associate professor of English at the University of Chicago.

ACKNOWLEDGEMENTS

The publisher thanks the following for their kind permission to reprint the work contained in this volume:

"Happy Birthday Moon," "Jamaican British," "The Perseverance," "Doctor Marigold Re-evaluated," "To Sweeten Bitter," and "Maybe I Could Love a Man" from *The Perseverance* by Raymond Antrobus are reprinted by permission of Penned in the Margins.

"Lake Michigan, Scene 1," "Lake Michigan, Scene 3," "Lake Michigan, Scene 6," and "Lake Michigan, Scene 18" from *Lake Michigan* by Daniel Borzutzky are reprinted by permission of University of Pittsburgh Press.

"Commute (Day One)," "After You're Gone (Day Six)," "Everyday Everyday Everyday (Day Nine)," "Winter's Smile (Day Nineteen)," "I Want to Go to the Island (Day Twenty)," "Underworld (Day Forty-Five)," and "Don't (Day Forty-Nine)" from *Autobiography of Death* by Kim Hyesoon, translated by Don Mee Choi, are reprinted by permission of New Directions.

"Almost Yesterday," "History Class," "January 1, Dawn," "Fishermen's Village," "This Gesture," and "The Stairs" from *Negative Space* by Luljeta Lleshanaku, translated by Ani Gjika, are reprinted by permission of Bloodaxe Books.

"Verso 1.1.01," "Verso 4," "Verso 32.2," "Verso 40.6," "Verso 55," and "Verso 33.1" (coda) from *The Blue Clerk* by Dionne Brand are reprinted by permission of McClelland & Stewart.

"We met at a birthday party . . . ," "The rain has stopped . . . ," "My mother was . . . ," "You knock on the door . . . ," "Darkness arrives without . . . ," "A five-year-old asks . . . ," "Riding home . . . ," "He'll just slip away . . . ," and "The horses, when I . . . ," from *Quarrels* by Eve Joseph are reprinted by permission of Anvil Press.

"Poem 10," "Poem 30," "Poem 39," "Poem 60," "Poem 67," "Poem 73," "Poem 74," and "Poem 89" from *The Art of Dying* by Sarah Tolmie are reprinted by permission of McGill-Queen's University Press.

THE GRIFFIN POETRY PRIZE
ANTHOLOGY 2019

The best books of poetry published in English internationally and in Canada are honoured each year with the $65,000 Griffin Poetry Prize, one of the world's most prestigious and richest international literary awards. Since 2001 this annual prize has acted as a tremendous spur to interest in and recognition of poetry, focusing worldwide attention on the formidable talent of poets writing in English and works in translation. And each year the editor of *The Griffin Poetry Prize Anthology* gathers the work of the extraordinary poets shortlisted for the awards, and introduces us to some of the finest poems in their collections.

This year, editor and prize juror Kim Maltman's selections from the international shortlist include poems from Raymond Antrobus's *The Perseverance* (Penned in the Margins), Daniel Borzutzky's *Lake Michigan* (University of Pittsburgh Press), Kim Hyesoon's *Autobiography of Death*, translated by Don Mee Choi (New Directions), and Luljeta Lleshanaku's *Negative Space*, translated by Ani Gjika (Bloodaxe Books). The selections from the Canadian shortlist include Dionne Brand's *The Blue Clerk* (McClelland & Stewart), Eve Joseph's *Quarrels* (Anvil Press), and Sarah Tolmie's *The Art of Dying* (McGill-Queen's University Press).

In choosing the 2019 shortlist, prize jurors Ulrikka Gernes, Srikanth Reddy, and Kim Maltman each read 510 books of poetry, from 32 countries, including 37 translations. The jurors also wrote the citations that introduce the seven poets' nominated works.

The Griffin Trust

Mark Doty
Carolyn Forché
Scott Griffin
Marek Kazmierski
Jo Shapcott
Karen Solie
Ian Williams
David Young

Trustees Emeriti

Margaret Atwood
Robert Hass
Michael Ondaatje
Robin Robertson
Colm Tóibín